NAME

CONTACT INFORMATION

ONE-EIGHTY

6-MONTH PLANNER

BroadStreet
PUBLISHING

BroadStreet Publishing Group LLC
Savage, Minnesota, USA
Broadstreetpublishing.com

ONE-EIGHTY PLANNER

ISBN 978-1-4245-5819-3

Design by Chris Garborg | garborgdesign.com
Compiled and edited by Michelle Winger | literallyprecise.com

Printed in China.

19 20 21 22 23 24 25 7 6 5 4 3 2 1

INTRODUCTION

Having trouble fitting everything in your day? This open 6-month planner makes getting organized simple and inspiring.

With undated monthly and weekly calendars, you are free to create your schedule and utilize this planner the way that makes the most sense to you. Use the space provided for daily goal setting and prioritizing. Encouraging Scriptures invite you to reflect on truth and find joy in the middle of your busy schedule.

Stay organized and be encouraged as you plan your days and spend moments with God.

MONTH

SUNDAY	MONDAY	TUESDAY	WEDNESDAY

NOTES

THURSDAY	FRIDAY	SATURDAY	ACTION POINTS

MONTH

SUNDAY	MONDAY	TUESDAY	WEDNESDAY

NOTES

THURSDAY	FRIDAY	SATURDAY	ACTION POINTS

MONTH ____________________

SUNDAY	MONDAY	TUESDAY	WEDNESDAY

NOTES

THURSDAY	FRIDAY	SATURDAY	ACTION POINTS

MONTH

SUNDAY	MONDAY	TUESDAY	WEDNESDAY

NOTES

THURSDAY	FRIDAY	SATURDAY	ACTION POINTS

MONTH

SUNDAY	MONDAY	TUESDAY	WEDNESDAY

NOTES

THURSDAY	FRIDAY	SATURDAY	ACTION POINTS

MONTH

SUNDAY	MONDAY	TUESDAY	WEDNESDAY

NOTES

THURSDAY FRIDAY SATURDAY

ACTION POINTS

WEEK

MONDAY

TUESDAY

WEDNESDAY

"For I know the plans I have for you," declares the Lord,
"plans to prosper you and not to harm you,
plans to give you hope and a future."

JEREMIAH 29:11 NIV

THURSDAY

FRIDAY

SATURDAY

SUNDAY

PRIORITIES

1.

2.

3.

DATE

I'M GRATEFUL FOR

NOTES

GOALS

DATE

PRIORITIES

1.

2.

3.

I'M GRATEFUL FOR

NOTES

GOALS

PRIORITIES

1.

2.

3.

DATE

I'M GRATEFUL FOR

NOTES

GOALS

DATE

I'M GRATEFUL FOR

PRIORITIES

1.

2.

3.

NOTES

GOALS

PRIORITIES

1.

2.

3.

DATE

I'M GRATEFUL FOR

NOTES

GOALS

DATE

I'M GRATEFUL FOR

PRIORITIES

1.

2.

3.

NOTES

GOALS

WEEK

MONDAY	TUESDAY	WEDNESDAY

I can do all this through him who gives me strength.

PHILIPPIANS 4:13 NIV

THURSDAY

FRIDAY

SATURDAY

SUNDAY

PRIORITIES

1.

2.

3.

DATE

I'M GRATEFUL FOR

NOTES

GOALS

DATE

PRIORITIES

1.

2.

3.

I'M GRATEFUL FOR

NOTES

GOALS

PRIORITIES

1.

2.

3.

DATE

I'M GRATEFUL FOR

NOTES

GOALS

DATE

PRIORITIES

1.

2.

3.

I'M GRATEFUL FOR

NOTES

GOALS

PRIORITIES

1.

2.

3.

DATE

I'M GRATEFUL FOR

NOTES

GOALS

DATE

I'M GRATEFUL FOR

PRIORITIES

1.

2.

3.

NOTES

GOALS

WEEK

MONDAY	TUESDAY	WEDNESDAY

Rejoice in the Lord always. I will say it again: Rejoice!
PHILIPPIANS 4:4 NIV

THURSDAY

FRIDAY

SATURDAY

SUNDAY

PRIORITIES

1.

2.

3.

DATE

I'M GRATEFUL FOR

NOTES

GOALS

DATE

I'M GRATEFUL FOR

PRIORITIES

1.

2.

3.

NOTES

GOALS

PRIORITIES

1.

2.

3.

DATE

I'M GRATEFUL FOR

NOTES

GOALS

DATE

I'M GRATEFUL FOR

PRIORITIES

1.

2.

3.

NOTES

GOALS

PRIORITIES

1.

2.

3.

DATE

I'M GRATEFUL FOR

NOTES

GOALS

DATE

I'M GRATEFUL FOR

PRIORITIES

1.

2.

3.

NOTES

GOALS

WEEK

MONDAY	TUESDAY	WEDNESDAY

You're the only place of protection for me.
I keep coming back to hide myself in you, for you are
like a mountain-cliff fortress where I am kept safe.

PSALM 71:3 TPT

THURSDAY

FRIDAY

SATURDAY

SUNDAY

PRIORITIES

1.

2.

3.

DATE

I'M GRATEFUL FOR

NOTES

GOALS

DATE

I'M GRATEFUL FOR

PRIORITIES

1.

2.

3.

NOTES

GOALS

PRIORITIES

1.

2.

3.

DATE

I'M GRATEFUL FOR

NOTES

GOALS

DATE

I'M GRATEFUL FOR

PRIORITIES

1.

2.

3.

NOTES

GOALS

PRIORITIES

1.

2.

3.

DATE

I'M GRATEFUL FOR

NOTES

GOALS

DATE

I'M GRATEFUL FOR

PRIORITIES

1.

2.

3.

NOTES

GOALS

WEEK

MONDAY	TUESDAY	WEDNESDAY

"Be still, and know that I am God. I will be exalted among the nations, I will be exalted in the earth!"

PSALM 46:10 ESV

THURSDAY

FRIDAY

SATURDAY

SUNDAY

PRIORITIES

1.

2.

3.

DATE

I'M GRATEFUL FOR

NOTES

GOALS

DATE

I'M GRATEFUL FOR

PRIORITIES

1.

2.

3.

NOTES

GOALS

PRIORITIES

1.

2.

3.

DATE

I'M GRATEFUL FOR

NOTES

GOALS

DATE

PRIORITIES

1.

2.

3.

I'M GRATEFUL FOR

NOTES

GOALS

PRIORITIES

1.

2.

3.

DATE

I'M GRATEFUL FOR

NOTES

GOALS

DATE

PRIORITIES

1.

2.

3.

I'M GRATEFUL FOR

NOTES

GOALS

WEEK

MONDAY	TUESDAY	WEDNESDAY

Within your heart you can make plans for your future,
but the Lord chooses the steps you take to get there.
PROVERBS 16:9 TPT

THURSDAY

FRIDAY

SATURDAY

SUNDAY

PRIORITIES

1.

2.

3.

DATE

I'M GRATEFUL FOR

NOTES

GOALS

DATE

I'M GRATEFUL FOR

PRIORITIES

1.

2.

3.

NOTES

GOALS

PRIORITIES

1.

2.

3.

DATE

I'M GRATEFUL FOR

NOTES

GOALS

DATE

PRIORITIES

1.

2.

3.

I'M GRATEFUL FOR

NOTES

GOALS

PRIORITIES

1.

2.

3.

DATE

I'M GRATEFUL FOR

NOTES

GOALS

DATE

PRIORITIES

1.

2.

3.

I'M GRATEFUL FOR

NOTES

GOALS

WEEK

MONDAY	TUESDAY	WEDNESDAY

Give all your worries and cares to God, for he cares for you.

1 PETER 5:7 NLT

THURSDAY

FRIDAY

SATURDAY

SUNDAY

PRIORITIES

1.

2.

3.

DATE

I'M GRATEFUL FOR

NOTES

GOALS

DATE

PRIORITIES

1.

2.

3.

I'M GRATEFUL FOR

NOTES

GOALS

PRIORITIES

1.

2.

3.

DATE

I'M GRATEFUL FOR

NOTES

GOALS

DATE

I'M GRATEFUL FOR

PRIORITIES

1.

2.

3.

NOTES

GOALS

PRIORITIES

1.

2.

3.

DATE

I'M GRATEFUL FOR

NOTES

GOALS

DATE

PRIORITIES

1.

2.

3.

I'M GRATEFUL FOR

NOTES

GOALS

WEEK

MONDAY

TUESDAY

WEDNESDAY

Watch your words and be careful what you say,
and you'll be surprised how few troubles you'll have.

PROVERBS 21:23 TPT

THURSDAY

FRIDAY

SATURDAY

SUNDAY

PRIORITIES

1.

2.

3.

DATE

I'M GRATEFUL FOR

NOTES

GOALS

DATE

I'M GRATEFUL FOR

PRIORITIES

1.

2.

3.

NOTES

GOALS

PRIORITIES

1.

2.

3.

DATE

I'M GRATEFUL FOR

NOTES

GOALS

DATE

I'M GRATEFUL FOR

PRIORITIES

1.

2.

3.

NOTES

GOALS

PRIORITIES

1.

2.

3.

DATE

I'M GRATEFUL FOR

NOTES

GOALS

DATE

I'M GRATEFUL FOR

PRIORITIES

1.

2.

3.

NOTES

GOALS

WEEK

MONDAY	TUESDAY	WEDNESDAY

This is the confidence we have in approaching God:
that if we ask anything according to his will, he hears us.

1 JOHN 5:14 NIV

THURSDAY	FRIDAY	SATURDAY
		SUNDAY

PRIORITIES

1.

2.

3.

DATE

I'M GRATEFUL FOR

NOTES

GOALS

DATE

PRIORITIES

1.

2.

3.

I'M GRATEFUL FOR

NOTES

GOALS

PRIORITIES

1.

2.

3.

DATE

I'M GRATEFUL FOR

NOTES

GOALS

DATE

PRIORITIES

1.

2.

3.

I'M GRATEFUL FOR

NOTES

GOALS

PRIORITIES

1.

2.

3.

DATE

I'M GRATEFUL FOR

NOTES

GOALS

DATE

PRIORITIES

1.

2.

3.

I'M GRATEFUL FOR

NOTES

GOALS

WEEK

MONDAY	TUESDAY	WEDNESDAY

May God, the inspiration and fountain of hope,
fill you to overflowing with uncontainable joy
and perfect peace as you trust in him.

ROMANS 15:13 TPT

THURSDAY

FRIDAY

SATURDAY

SUNDAY

PRIORITIES

1.

2.

3.

DATE

I'M GRATEFUL FOR

NOTES

GOALS

DATE

I'M GRATEFUL FOR

PRIORITIES

1.

2.

3.

NOTES

GOALS

PRIORITIES

1.

2.

3.

DATE

I'M GRATEFUL FOR

NOTES

GOALS

DATE

I'M GRATEFUL FOR

PRIORITIES

1.

2.

3.

NOTES

GOALS

PRIORITIES

1.

2.

3.

DATE

I'M GRATEFUL FOR

NOTES

GOALS

DATE

PRIORITIES

1.

2.

3.

I'M GRATEFUL FOR

NOTES

GOALS

WEEK

MONDAY	TUESDAY	WEDNESDAY

There is no fear in love. But perfect love drives out fear, because fear has to do with punishment. The one who fears is not made perfect in love.

1 JOHN 4:18 NIV

THURSDAY

FRIDAY

SATURDAY

SUNDAY

PRIORITIES

1.

2.

3.

DATE

I'M GRATEFUL FOR

NOTES

GOALS

DATE

I'M GRATEFUL FOR

PRIORITIES

1.

2.

3.

NOTES

GOALS

PRIORITIES

1.

2.

3.

DATE

I'M GRATEFUL FOR

NOTES

GOALS

DATE

I'M GRATEFUL FOR

PRIORITIES

1.

2.

3.

NOTES

GOALS

PRIORITIES

1.

2.

3.

DATE

I'M GRATEFUL FOR

NOTES

GOALS

DATE

I'M GRATEFUL FOR

PRIORITIES

1.

2.

3.

NOTES

GOALS

WEEK

MONDAY	TUESDAY	WEDNESDAY

Put your heart and soul into every activity you do,
as though you are doing it for the Lord himself
and not merely for others.

COLOSSIANS 3:23 TPT

THURSDAY

FRIDAY

SATURDAY

SUNDAY

PRIORITIES

1.

2.

3.

DATE

I'M GRATEFUL FOR

NOTES

GOALS

DATE

PRIORITIES

1.

2.

3.

I'M GRATEFUL FOR

NOTES

GOALS

PRIORITIES

1.

2.

3.

DATE

I'M GRATEFUL FOR

NOTES

GOALS

DATE

I'M GRATEFUL FOR

PRIORITIES

1.

2.

3.

NOTES

GOALS

PRIORITIES

1.

2.

3.

DATE

I'M GRATEFUL FOR

NOTES

GOALS

DATE

PRIORITIES

1.

2.

3.

I'M GRATEFUL FOR

NOTES

GOALS

WEEK

MONDAY	TUESDAY	WEDNESDAY

The LORD directs the steps of the godly.
He delights in every detail of their lives.
PSALM 37:23 NLT

THURSDAY

FRIDAY

SATURDAY

SUNDAY

PRIORITIES

1.

2.

3.

DATE

I'M GRATEFUL FOR

NOTES

GOALS

DATE

I'M GRATEFUL FOR

PRIORITIES

1.

2.

3.

NOTES

GOALS

PRIORITIES

1.

2.

3.

DATE

I'M GRATEFUL FOR

NOTES

GOALS

DATE

I'M GRATEFUL FOR

PRIORITIES

1.

2.

3.

NOTES

GOALS

PRIORITIES

1.

2.

3.

DATE

I'M GRATEFUL FOR

NOTES

GOALS

DATE

I'M GRATEFUL FOR

PRIORITIES

1.

2.

3.

NOTES

GOALS

WEEK

MONDAY

TUESDAY

WEDNESDAY

"Does worry add anything to your life?
Can it add one more year, or even one day?"

LUKE 12:25 TPT

THURSDAY	FRIDAY	SATURDAY

SUNDAY

PRIORITIES

1.

2.

3.

DATE

I'M GRATEFUL FOR

NOTES

GOALS

DATE

PRIORITIES

1.

2.

3.

I'M GRATEFUL FOR

NOTES

GOALS

PRIORITIES

1.

2.

3.

DATE

I'M GRATEFUL FOR

NOTES

GOALS

DATE

PRIORITIES

1.

2.

3.

I'M GRATEFUL FOR

NOTES

GOALS

PRIORITIES

1.

2.

3.

DATE

I'M GRATEFUL FOR

NOTES

GOALS

DATE

I'M GRATEFUL FOR

PRIORITIES

1.

2.

3.

NOTES

GOALS

WEEK

MONDAY	TUESDAY	WEDNESDAY

"You will know the truth, and the truth will set you free."

JOHN 8:32 ESV

THURSDAY

FRIDAY

SATURDAY

SUNDAY

PRIORITIES

1.

2.

3.

DATE

I'M GRATEFUL FOR

NOTES

GOALS

DATE

I'M GRATEFUL FOR

PRIORITIES

1.

2.

3.

NOTES

GOALS

PRIORITIES

1.

2.

3.

DATE

I'M GRATEFUL FOR

NOTES

GOALS

DATE

I'M GRATEFUL FOR

PRIORITIES

1.

2.

3.

NOTES

GOALS

PRIORITIES

1.

2.

3.

DATE

I'M GRATEFUL FOR

NOTES

GOALS

DATE

I'M GRATEFUL FOR

PRIORITIES

1.

2.

3.

NOTES

GOALS

WEEK

MONDAY	TUESDAY	WEDNESDAY

Truthful words will stand the test of time,
but one day every lie will be seen for what it is.
PROVERBS 12:19 TPT

THURSDAY

FRIDAY

SATURDAY

SUNDAY

PRIORITIES

1.

2.

3.

DATE

I'M GRATEFUL FOR

NOTES

GOALS

DATE

PRIORITIES

1.

2.

3.

I'M GRATEFUL FOR

NOTES

GOALS

PRIORITIES

1.

2.

3.

DATE

I'M GRATEFUL FOR

NOTES

GOALS

DATE

PRIORITIES

1.

2.

3.

I'M GRATEFUL FOR

NOTES

GOALS

PRIORITIES

1.

2.

3.

DATE

I'M GRATEFUL FOR

NOTES

GOALS

DATE

I'M GRATEFUL FOR

PRIORITIES

1.

2.

3.

NOTES

GOALS

WEEK

MONDAY	TUESDAY	WEDNESDAY

Give thanks in all circumstances; for this is the will of God in Christ Jesus for you.

1 THESSALONIANS 5:18 ESV

THURSDAY

FRIDAY

SATURDAY

SUNDAY

PRIORITIES

1.

2.

3.

DATE

I'M GRATEFUL FOR

NOTES

GOALS

DATE

PRIORITIES

1.

2.

3.

I'M GRATEFUL FOR

NOTES

GOALS

PRIORITIES

1.

2.

3.

DATE

I'M GRATEFUL FOR

NOTES

GOALS

DATE

PRIORITIES

1.

2.

3.

I'M GRATEFUL FOR

NOTES

GOALS

PRIORITIES

1.

2.

3.

DATE

I'M GRATEFUL FOR

NOTES

GOALS

DATE

PRIORITIES

1.

2.

3.

I'M GRATEFUL FOR

NOTES

GOALS

WEEK

MONDAY	TUESDAY	WEDNESDAY

We know that in all things God works for the good of those who love him, who have been called according to his purpose.

ROMANS 8:28 NIV

THURSDAY

FRIDAY

SATURDAY

SUNDAY

PRIORITIES

1.

2.

3.

DATE

I'M GRATEFUL FOR

NOTES

GOALS

DATE

I'M GRATEFUL FOR

PRIORITIES

1.

2.

3.

NOTES

GOALS

PRIORITIES

1.

2.

3.

DATE

I'M GRATEFUL FOR

NOTES

GOALS

DATE

I'M GRATEFUL FOR

PRIORITIES

1.

2.

3.

NOTES

GOALS

PRIORITIES

1.

2.

3.

DATE

I'M GRATEFUL FOR

NOTES

GOALS

DATE

I'M GRATEFUL FOR

PRIORITIES

1.

2.

3.

NOTES

GOALS

WEEK

MONDAY	TUESDAY	WEDNESDAY

Let the sunrise of your love end our dark night. Break through our clouded dawn again! Only you can satisfy our hearts, filling us with songs of joy to the end of our days.

PSALM 90:14 TPT

THURSDAY

FRIDAY

SATURDAY

SUNDAY

PRIORITIES

1.

2.

3.

DATE

I'M GRATEFUL FOR

NOTES

GOALS

DATE

I'M GRATEFUL FOR

PRIORITIES

1.

2.

3.

NOTES

GOALS

PRIORITIES

1.

2.

3.

DATE

I'M GRATEFUL FOR

NOTES

GOALS

DATE

I'M GRATEFUL FOR

PRIORITIES

1.

2.

3.

NOTES

GOALS

PRIORITIES

1.

2.

3.

DATE

I'M GRATEFUL FOR

NOTES

GOALS

DATE

I'M GRATEFUL FOR

PRIORITIES

1.

2.

3.

NOTES

GOALS

WEEK

MONDAY	TUESDAY	WEDNESDAY

Let's not get tired of doing what is good.
At just the right time we will reap a
harvest of blessing if we don't give up.

GALATIANS 6:9 NLT

THURSDAY

FRIDAY

SATURDAY

SUNDAY

PRIORITIES

1.

2.

3.

DATE

I'M GRATEFUL FOR

NOTES

GOALS

DATE

PRIORITIES

1.

2.

3.

I'M GRATEFUL FOR

NOTES

GOALS

PRIORITIES

1.

2.

3.

DATE

I'M GRATEFUL FOR

NOTES

GOALS

DATE

PRIORITIES

1.

2.

3.

I'M GRATEFUL FOR

NOTES

GOALS

PRIORITIES

1.

2.

3.

DATE

I'M GRATEFUL FOR

NOTES

GOALS

DATE

I'M GRATEFUL FOR

PRIORITIES

1.

2.

3.

NOTES

GOALS

WEEK

MONDAY	TUESDAY	WEDNESDAY

Those who hope in the Lord will renew their strength.
They will soar on wings like eagles; they will run
and not grow weary, they will walk and not be faint.

ISAIAH 40:31 NIV

THURSDAY

FRIDAY

SATURDAY

SUNDAY

PRIORITIES

1.

2.

3.

DATE

I'M GRATEFUL FOR

NOTES

GOALS

DATE

I'M GRATEFUL FOR

PRIORITIES

1.

2.

3.

NOTES

GOALS

PRIORITIES

1.

2.

3.

DATE

I'M GRATEFUL FOR

NOTES

GOALS

DATE

I'M GRATEFUL FOR

PRIORITIES

1.

2.

3.

NOTES

GOALS

PRIORITIES

1.

2.

3.

DATE

I'M GRATEFUL FOR

NOTES

GOALS

DATE

PRIORITIES

1.

2.

3.

I'M GRATEFUL FOR

NOTES

GOALS

WEEK

MONDAY	TUESDAY	WEDNESDAY

If your faith remains strong, even while surrounded by life's difficulties, you will continue to experience the untold blessings of God!

JAMES 1:12 TPT

THURSDAY

FRIDAY

SATURDAY

SUNDAY

PRIORITIES

1.

2.

3.

DATE

I'M GRATEFUL FOR

NOTES

GOALS

DATE

I'M GRATEFUL FOR

PRIORITIES

1.

2.

3.

NOTES

GOALS

PRIORITIES

1.

2.

3.

DATE

I'M GRATEFUL FOR

NOTES

GOALS

DATE

PRIORITIES

1.

2.

3.

I'M GRATEFUL FOR

NOTES

GOALS

PRIORITIES

1.

2.

3.

DATE

I'M GRATEFUL FOR

NOTES

GOALS

DATE

I'M GRATEFUL FOR

PRIORITIES

1.

2.

3.

NOTES

GOALS

WEEK

MONDAY	TUESDAY	WEDNESDAY

Trust in the LORD with all your heart; do not depend on your own understanding. Seek his will in all you do, and he will show you which path to take.

PROVERBS 3:5-6 NLT

THURSDAY

FRIDAY

SATURDAY

SUNDAY

PRIORITIES

1.

2.

3.

DATE

I'M GRATEFUL FOR

NOTES

GOALS

DATE

I'M GRATEFUL FOR

PRIORITIES

1.

2.

3.

NOTES

GOALS

PRIORITIES

1.

2.

3.

DATE

I'M GRATEFUL FOR

NOTES

GOALS

DATE

I'M GRATEFUL FOR

PRIORITIES

1.

2.

3.

NOTES

GOALS

PRIORITIES

1.

2.

3.

DATE

I'M GRATEFUL FOR

NOTES

GOALS

DATE

I'M GRATEFUL FOR

PRIORITIES

1.

2.

3.

NOTES

GOALS

WEEK

MONDAY	TUESDAY	WEDNESDAY

"Be strong and courageous. Do not be afraid;
do not be discouraged, for the LORD your God
will be with you wherever you go."

JOSHUA 1:9 NIV

THURSDAY

FRIDAY

SATURDAY

SUNDAY

PRIORITIES

1.

2.

3.

DATE

I'M GRATEFUL FOR

NOTES

GOALS

DATE

PRIORITIES

1.

2.

3.

I'M GRATEFUL FOR

NOTES

GOALS

PRIORITIES

1.

2.

3.

DATE

I'M GRATEFUL FOR

NOTES

GOALS

DATE

PRIORITIES

1.

2.

3.

I'M GRATEFUL FOR

NOTES

GOALS

PRIORITIES

1.

2.

3.

DATE

I'M GRATEFUL FOR

NOTES

GOALS

DATE

PRIORITIES

1.

2.

3.

I'M GRATEFUL FOR

NOTES

GOALS

WEEK

MONDAY	TUESDAY	WEDNESDAY

"I have told you these things, so that in me you may have peace. In this world you will have trouble. But take heart! I have overcome the world."

JOHN 16:33 NIV

THURSDAY

FRIDAY

SATURDAY

SUNDAY

PRIORITIES

1. ______________________

____

2. ______________________

____

3. ______________________

____

DATE ______________________

I'M GRATEFUL FOR

____

____

____

____

____

____

NOTES

GOALS

DATE

I'M GRATEFUL FOR

PRIORITIES

1.

2.

3.

NOTES

GOALS

PRIORITIES

1.

2.

3.

DATE

I'M GRATEFUL FOR

NOTES

GOALS

DATE

PRIORITIES

1.

2.

3.

I'M GRATEFUL FOR

NOTES

GOALS

PRIORITIES

1.

2.

3.

DATE

I'M GRATEFUL FOR

NOTES

GOALS

DATE

PRIORITIES

1.

2.

3.

I'M GRATEFUL FOR

NOTES

GOALS

WEEK

MONDAY	TUESDAY	WEDNESDAY

O Lord, you alone are my hope.
I've trusted you, O Lord, from childhood.
PSALM 71:5 NLT

THURSDAY

FRIDAY

SATURDAY

SUNDAY

PRIORITIES

1.

2.

3.

DATE

I'M GRATEFUL FOR

NOTES

GOALS

DATE

I'M GRATEFUL FOR

PRIORITIES

1.

2.

3.

NOTES

GOALS

PRIORITIES

1.

2.

3.

DATE

I'M GRATEFUL FOR

NOTES

GOALS

DATE

PRIORITIES

1.

2.

3.

I'M GRATEFUL FOR

NOTES

GOALS

PRIORITIES

1.

2.

3.

DATE

I'M GRATEFUL FOR

NOTES

GOALS

DATE

I'M GRATEFUL FOR

PRIORITIES

1.

2.

3.

NOTES

GOALS

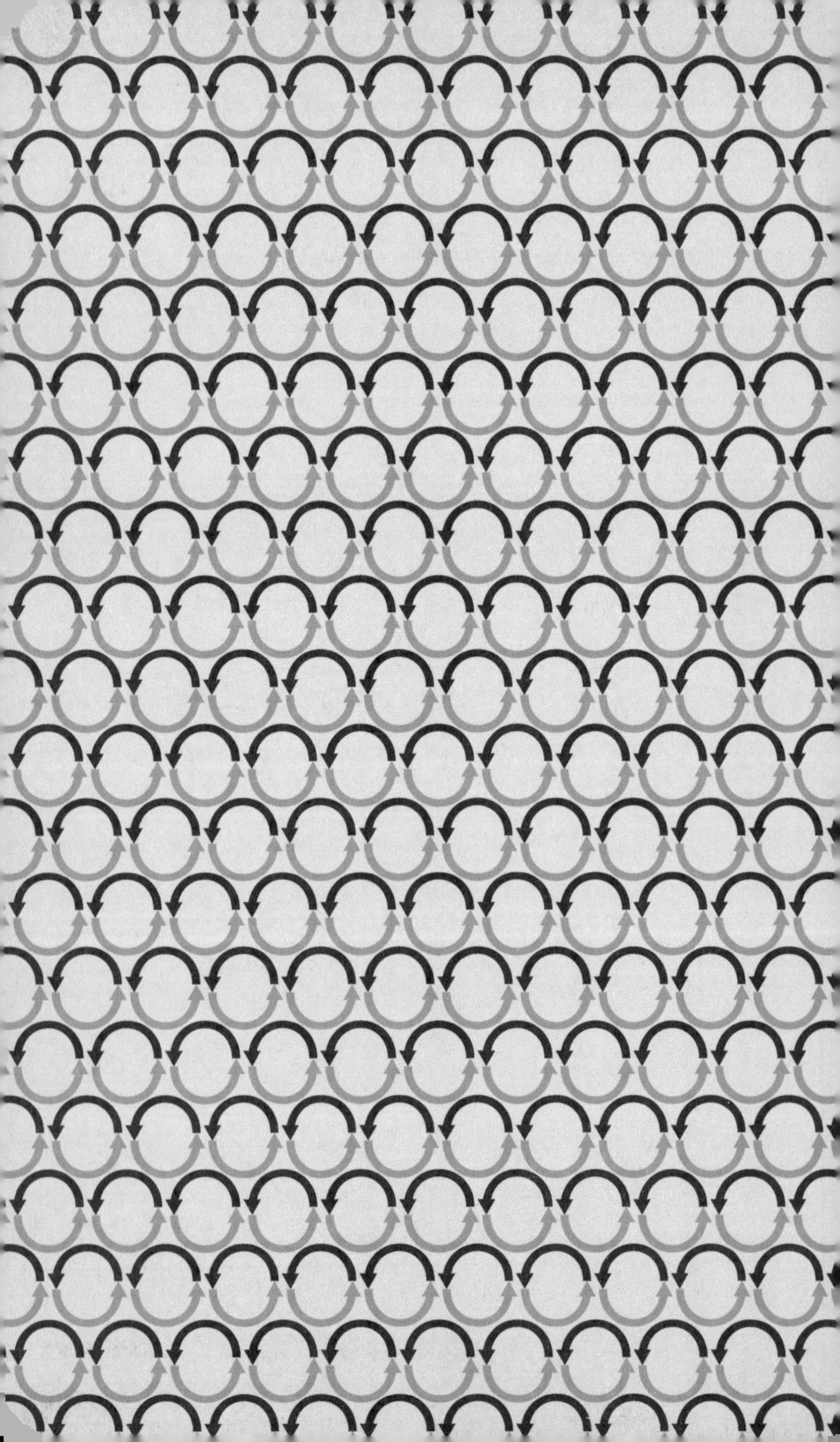